Welcome to Father Time!

One of the first important lessons that I learned when I became a new dad was that my child would need my love, nurturance and support "around the clock." Indeed, good dads engage their kids physically, emotionally and spiritually. In a practical sense, that means that they provide, nurture and guide their children. Truly, the rewarding work of being a dad is never done. It's an exhilarating "24/7" commitment that challenges every dad to be the best dad that he can be. That's why I am so excited about our **24/7 Dad**™ program. It provides the around the clock support that every dad needs.

24/7 Dad™ is a unique and innovative fatherhood program developed by a team of nationally and internationally recognized fathering experts and fatherhood practitioners. The **24/7 Dad**™ program focuses on characteristics that every father needs and covers the universal aspects of fatherhood so that men of all cultures, races, religions, and backgrounds can benefit from the program. You will hone your fathering skills as you learn about yourself and the important roles that you have with your children and in your family. In addition, you will learn important ways to strengthen your relationship with your wife or with the mother of your children. Finally, you will be given a great opportunity to develop effective strategies to manage your physical and mental health and to help you balance your work and family commitments.

When I said that the **24/7 Dad**™ program was comprehensive, I wasn't kidding. But it needs to be. After all, the health and well-being of your children is at stake. (Frankly, I am a bit envious that a fathering program like this was not available before I changed my first diaper!) So wind your "fatherhood time piece" and get ready to embark on the exciting and rewarding journey—the journey to become a 24/7 dad. And always remember that "father time is all the time when you are somebody's dad!"

Best regards,

Roland C. Warren

Roland Warren
President
National Fatherhood Initiative

To Learn More About NFI and the *24/7 Dad*™ Programs:

TRAINING, TECHNICAL ASSISTANCE AND QUESTIONS ABOUT THE 24/7 DAD™ PROGRAMS

Phone: (301) 948-0599
Fax: (301) 948-4325
Email: community@fatherhood.org
Website: www.fatherhood.org

LEARN MORE ABOUT NATIONAL FATHERHOOD INITIATIVE

101 Lake Forest Boulevard, Suite 360
Gaithersburg, MD 20877

Phone: (301) 948-0599
Fax: (301) 948-4325
Email: info@fatherhood.org
Website: www.fatherhood.org

National Fatherhood Initiative℠

First Edition
Christopher Brown, John Chacón, and Karen Patterson
With contributions from Stephen Bavolek, Ph.D., CEO & Founder of Family Development Resources, Inc.

© 2004 National Fatherhood Initiative   Printed in the United States of America.

ATTENTION: Trademark and Copyright Protection
The manuals, inventories and other instructional materials published by the National Fatherhood Initiative are federally protected against unauthorized reproduction whether print or electronic.

FATHERING HANDBOOK

FATHERING HANDBOOK

www.fatherhood.org

First Edition ©2004 National Fatherhood Initiative

National Fatherhood Initiative

24/7 Dad P.M.™ Program

FATHERING HANDBOOK

TABLE OF CONTENTS

I.	Session 1 Fathering and the 24/7 Dad	1
II.	Session 2 Growing from Boyhood to Manhood	4
III.	Session 3 Recognizing and Handling Feelings of Anger	9
IV.	Session 4 What It Means to Be a Man	13
V.	Session 5 Spirituality and Growth	16
VI.	Session 6 Sex, Love, and Relationships	21
VII.	Session 7 Power and Control	25
VIII.	Session 8 Competition and Fathering	28
IX.	Session 9 Improving My Communication Skills	31
X.	Session 10 Having Fun and Getting Involved	35
XI.	Session 11 Stress, Alcohol, and Work	39
XII.	Session 12 Growth and Celebration	43

Session 1
Fathering and the 24/7 Dad

The 24/7 Dad™ Program is based on the five traits of the ideal father.

Self-Awareness
The 24/7 Dad is aware of himself as a man and aware of how important he is to his family. He is in touch with his moods, feelings, and emotions. He knows his strengths and limits. The 24/7 Dad takes responsibility for his own actions and knows that his growth depends on how well he knows and accepts himself.

The 24/7 Dad asks himself:
"How well am I doing in knowing myself?"

Caring for Self
The 24/7 Dad takes care of himself. He goes for yearly check-ups, eats the right foods, exercises, and learns new facts about the world he lives in. He has a strong spiritual connection to his community and chooses friends that support his healthy choices. The 24/7 Dad models behaviors for his children that clearly show he respects and likes himself by making good choices.

The 24/7 Dad asks himself:
"How well am I doing in taking care of myself?"

Fathering Skills
Fathering is a man's unique ability to contribute to the positive health and well-being of his children and family. The 24/7 Dad is very aware of the vital role he has in the family. He is a positive role model. He knows that fathers are involved in the daily life of their children. The 24/7 Dad gets his kids up, dressed, and fed in the mornings. He meets with his children's teachers and helps his children with homework. He supports his children's interests in sports and other activities. The 24/7 Dad knows that he and the mother of his children parent differently. In other words, he knows the difference between "fathering" and "mothering" and how that difference is good for his children.

The 24/7 Dad asks himself:
"How well am I doing in being a Father?"

Parenting Skills
Parenting is the knowledge and skills that dads and moms need to raise healthy, happy children. The 24/7 Dad nurtures his children. He knows and accepts how vital his parenting skills are to developing the physical, emotional, intellectual, social, spiritual, and creative needs of his children. The 24/7 Dad creates a positive, trusting home where children grow with the support and love of dad who cares for and nurtures them. A 24/7 Dad knows that discipline teaches and guides children, and is not used to physically and emotionally threaten or harm them.

The 24/7 Dad asks himself:
"How well am I doing in being a parent?"

Relationship Skills
The 24/7 Dad builds and maintains healthy relationships with his children, wife, family and friends, and community. He knows and values the power of relationships to shape the characters of his children, and the quality of life he has with his wife. He knows that how well he communicates, models proper behavior, and chooses healthy friends all help shape the lives of his family.

The 24/7 Dad asks himself:
"How well am I doing in my relationships?"

The Story About Me: My Life in a Nutshell

The name of the actor starring in this movie is
_____.
(Your Name)

The story begins in_____
(Place of Birth)
in the year_____.
(Date of Birth)

In the beginning, the major supporting actors in the story are_____.
(Childhood Family)

Today the major supporting actors are
_____
_____.
(Current Family)

This story is about a little boy who grows up believing_____
_____
and then finds out in later life that_____
_____.

There are many challenges in life faced by this boy and man, which include_____,
but the one most memorable scene takes place in _____ when_____
_____ happens.

What makes this scene so memorable is_____
_____.

Throughout life, the main character meets heroes like_____.
(People and/or Events)

and villains like_____.
(People and/or Events)

This ongoing story is heading toward _____.
And at the end of the story the critics will say
_____.

Being a 24/7 Dad

Rate yourself using a five-point scale on how well you are doing being a 24/7 Dad. Column 1 - rate yourself before you first became a father; Column 2 – six months to a year into fatherhood; Column 3 – where you are today. (Column 4 will be completed when you complete the program.)

Rating Scale: 0 = if you did not take part in the 24/7 Dad AM™ program (column 1 and 2 only)
1 = very low
2 = somewhat
3 = average
4 = pretty good
5 = very good

	Column 1 Pre "A.M." Sessions	Column 2 Post "A.M." Sessions	Column 3 Pre "P.M." Sessions	Column 4 Post "P.M." Sessions
a. Self-Awareness				
b. Caring for Self				
a. Fathering Skills				
a. Parenting Skills				

Weekly Activity Log

Session 1: Fathering and the 24/7 Dad

a. One new thing I learned today was _____
_____
_____
_____

b. This information will help me become a better dad because _____
_____
_____
_____

c. The "Action Steps" I need to take are:

    1. _____
_____

    2. _____
_____

    3. _____
_____

    4. _____
_____

FATHERING HANDBOOK • SESSION 2: GROWING FROM BOYHOOD TO MANHOOD

Session 2

Growing from Boyhood to Manhood

One way boys are a lot different from girls is

_____

_____

_____.

One way I was different from girls I knew growing up was_____

_____

_____

_____.

One way boys and girls are alike is_____

_____

_____

_____.

Male vs. Female Brains

1. **The brains of males are different from the brains of females.**
True. While male and female brains are set up with the same three parts (brainstem, limbic system, and neocortex), there is a difference in the size and function of male and female brains.

2. **The male brain tends to be geared for talking rather than for doing.**
False. Men tend to be better than women at tasks that require spatial skills, such as throwing and catching a ball and some forms of math. Surges of testosterone in the womb and at puberty help develop the male brain to perform these tasks.

3. **The brain secretes serotonin, which is a chemical that calms us down. Men have less serotonin than women.**
True. As a result, men tend to act more impulsively than women. Women, however, use their store of serotonin more quickly than men do and don't replace it as quickly as men do.

4. **Girls would rather play with dolls while boys would rather throw a ball around. This is learned behavior.**
True & False. The brains of girls generally secrete a higher level of oxytocin, a brain chemical that causes us to bond and feel empathic. Based on higher levels of serotonin (calming) and oxytocin (bonding), girls generally spend more time relating to others in a more calm way than boys. Boys tend to be more active and less verbal than girls. Social factors also play a role in these differences. We expect girls and boys to have different interests.

4   First Edition ©2004 National Fatherhood Initiative

www.fatherhood.org

5. Testosterone is the hormone related to higher levels of sexual energy and aggression in males.
True. Men have up to 20 times more testosterone than women.

6. Try as you might, females remember more than males.
True. The memory center in women is larger than in men.

7. Men's brains take different mental "naps" than women's brains.
True. Women's brains are constantly working. Men's brains "zone out" and take more mental naps (e.g. zoned out in front of the TV).

8. Some violence is intentional.
True. Brain chemicals that prepare the body for "fight or flight" play a major role in aggression and violence.

9. No matter what you do, males will be more aggressive than females.
False. The way that boys are raised can increase their ability to bond and decrease their tendency toward aggression.

Which of these above facts are true for you?

Self-Concept, Self-Esteem, and Self-Worth

Self-Concept
What you think of yourself

A man's self-concept is the thoughts he has about himself. For a man, a self-concept can be positive or negative thoughts about different aspects of his life. A man might have a positive self-concept of himself as a gardener, but a negative self-concept of himself as a cook. The self-concept of a man varies as widely as his roles and responsibilities. The man with an overall positive self-concept tends to thinks of himself in a positive way.

Self-Esteem
What you feel about yourself

A man's self-esteem is the feelings he has about himself. Overall, does a man hold himself in high esteem or low esteem? Messages we get from others help to shape to our self-esteem.

Self-Worth
The overall thoughts and feelings that a man has about himself.

The ways in which a man can build his self-worth are similar to the ways in which Dads can help build self-worth in their children.

Internal Mind Messages

Getting in touch with the negative and positive internal messages that we send ourselves is the first step in building self-worth.

Examples:

Negative
I'm not going to succeed.

Positive
I will succeed.

Negative
She won't like me. I'm not good enough.

Positive
Even if she doesn't like me, I'm a good man and I value and like myself.

What is a negative message you send yourself?

_____

_____

_____

The view we have of ourselves results from previous experiences, even as far back as childhood.

The mind forms habits in thinking. One way to break a "habit thought" is to think an opposite thought. Every time a negative message runs in your head, replace it with a positive message.

Change your negative message into a positive one and write it here:_____

_____

_____

Positive Reminders

Using small sticky notes, write positive words that reflect traits or behaviors you would like to develop. If you want to create a respectful relationship with your wife or children, write the word "respect" on sticky notes and place them in areas in your daily life that you frequent. It's best if you work on one trait or behavior at a time.

When you practice or show your desired trait, make a mark or star on your sticky note as a reward to yourself.

Do the same with behaviors or traits you want to encourage with other family members. Every time you see the trait or behavior, praise the person or the behavior, i.e. "Thanks for cooperating" (Praise for Behavior) or "You really are a special person." (Praise for Being).

Make a mark or star on the sticky note every time you see the desired trait or behavior. If you like, make a mark on another piece of paper of the times you saw an undesirable trait or behavior. Are you paying more attention to these behaviors? Work to change your pattern.

Praise for Being
"I love you son. You are very special to me." Practice giving "Praise for Being" statements to all family members every day.

Praise for Behavior
"You did a great job cleaning your room!" Practice giving "Praise for Behavior" statements to all family members every day.

Self-Praise
Remember to praise yourself for Being and for Doing every day.

Self-Praise for Being
"I'm a worthwhile person." "I'm a caring man."

Self-Praise for Doing
"I'm doing a good job of listening to others."
"I did a nice job cooking dinner."

And make it a habit to accept praise messages sent to you. A "thank you" is the polite way to receive and value a gift.

Nurturing Touch
Nurturing touch is a great way to build positive self-worth. Children love to be held and hugged, have their back rubbed, their hand held, love to sit on their parent's lap, etc. Give and get hugs daily. If you have older children (e.g. teenagers), remember that they need to receive nurturing touch just as much as a small child does. Because touch is a basic human need, men who give and receive hugs are meeting their basic need to be touched.

Giving nurturing touch is also vital in the positive development of children's brains. Research shows that gentle touch helps children form a gentler, patient brain. Hurting touch creates angry, impatient brains.

Experience Success
A good way to build self-worth as a man is to see what you are good at doing, and do more of it. If working on projects helps you feel successful, try to include the activity often in your life.

Be There for Others
A great way to build self-worth is to help others. Helping includes listening without interrupting, and valuing what another person has to say or believes, even if it's different from your beliefs. Helping also includes being there as a father with your children and being there as a husband to your wife/partner.

Which of the strategies above do you need to work on first?

Can you think of other ideas to help you build self-worth in yourself and your family?

Weekly Activity Log

Session 2: Growing from Boyhood to Manhood

a. One new thing I learned today was _____

_____

_____

_____

b. This information will help me become a better dad because _____

_____

_____

_____

c. The "Action Steps" I need to take are:

    1. _____

_____

    2. _____

_____

    3. _____

_____

    4. _____

_____

FATHERING HANDBOOK

Session 3
Recognizing and Handling Feelings of Anger

The model that I present to my children to express anger is_____
_____
_____
_____.

What I hope my children learn by watching me is_____
_____
_____
_____.

What I fear my children learn by watching me is
_____
_____
_____
_____.

Anger is a secondary emotion that is usually caused by past pain or hurt that is not expressed. The expression of the anger is the expression of the past hurt or pain.

Examples:

Your boss is critical of your work. You feel he is being unfair, but don't want to tell him that. You come home and yell at the children for not doing their homework.

What happened?

Your in-law or neighbor has been putting down the way you parent for years. You feel hurt, but don't say anything and just grin and bear it. One day he makes an innocent comment or joke and you explode.

What happened?

To me, the feeling of anger is (describe the feeling of anger)_____
_____
_____
_____

When I get angry, it usually is because
_____
_____
_____.

www.fatherhood.org

First Edition ©2004 National Fatherhood Initiative

FATHERING HANDBOOK • SESSION 3: RECOGNIZING AND HANDLING FEELINGS OF ANGER

Think about a few times when you've gotten angry. How did you handle your anger then? How do you handle your anger these days? In the same way? In a different way?

Some Facts and Myths About Anger

1. Men often find if harder to express their feelings of hurt than women.
Fact. Men often find it harder to express **all** feelings compared to women and children.

2. Boy babies are fussier, easer to excite, harder to calm down, and respond to change with less ease than girl babies.
Fact. Boy babies tend to be fussier, get excited more easily, are harder to calm down, and respond to change with less ease than girl babies. As a result, parents sometimes "hush" boys to be quiet and tell girls to be more expressive.

3. Boys are taught not to cry; girls are taught it's okay to cry.
Fact. Boys are usually taught to keep their tears inside. When a boy cries, it is often seen as a sign of weakness.

4. When boys express their anger, they tend to be more violent than girls.
Fact. Males tend to commit more violent crimes than females. Anger is the emotion that most often leads males to be violent.

• Boys are taught to express their anger energy aggressively, usually by hitting something.

• Boys are also taught to get angry and to take their anger out on their rivals in contact sports, such as boxing, wrestling, football, and hockey. The result is a high number of fights in male sporting events.

• Many girls, on the other hand, are taught not to express their anger at all. This creates lots of stress that could be related to anxiety and depression in females.

There are four goals in managing anger:

1. Be aware of feelings of hurt when they happen and express them properly at all times. When you suppress hurtful feelings or deny them, it only builds up anger energy inside.

2. Be aware of feelings of anger when they arise so that you can express your anger calmly.

3. Express the anger energy in proper ways. Don't hit, yell, call someone bad names, or abuse someone in any other way.

4. Teach your children how to express their anger properly by being a good role model.

How can you show your children (model) to properly express anger? Write three ways in which you can properly express your anger:

1._____

_____

_____

_____

2._____

_____

_____

_____

3._____

_____

_____

_____

Weekly Activity Log

Session 3: Recognizing and Handling Feelings of Anger

a. One new thing I learned today was _____

b. This information will help me become a better dad because _____

c. The "Action Steps" I need to take are:

   1. _____

   2. _____

   3. _____

   4. _____

FATHERING HANDBOOK

Session 4

What It Means to Be a Man

To me, being a man means_____
_____
_____.

The trait of being a man I most admire is_____
_____
_____.

The trait of being a man I least admire is_____
_____
_____.

Popular media (TV, movies, magazines, etc.) portrays different types of masculinity (what it means to be a man). Above each type, write which traits best describe "masculinity" for typical males in each category:

_____
Male Movie Actor

_____
Playboy

_____
NASCAR Driver

_____
Football Player

_____
Business CEO

_____
Politician

_____
Rock Musician

_____
Rapper

_____
Drill Sergeant

_____
Father

_____
Sports Announcer

_____
TV Actor playing lawyer, doctor, law enforcement officer, etc.

www.fatherhood.org

First Edition ©2004 National Fatherhood Initiative

FATHERING HANDBOOK • SESSION 4: WHAT IT MEANS TO BE A MAN

_____
Comedian

_____
Auto Assembly line Worker

_____
Male Clergy Member (priest, pastor, rabbi, etc.)

The concept of "masculinity" (what it means to be a man) is also learned from culture and family. Race, economic level, and education among other factors can play a part in how a culture defines masculinity.

In the 1980s, researchers identified a list of traits that were commonly associated with masculinity. These are:

Yesterday   **Me**
Self-confident   ____

Courageous   ____

Leadership   ____

Dependable   ____

Successful   ____

Self-Reliant   ____

Controlling (situations ____
or other people)

Identify seven characteristics that best describe masculinity today and write them below. Rate yourself on each of the seven characteristics using the 0 to 3 scale.

Today   **Me**

1. _____   ____

2. _____   ____

3. _____   ____

4. _____   ____

5. _____   ____

6. _____   ____

7. _____   ____

Identify seven traits that you would like to pass on to your son(s) or model for your daughter(s):

1. _____

2. _____

3. _____

4. _____

5. _____

6. _____

7. _____

First Edition ©2004 National Fatherhood Initiative   www.fatherhood.org

Weekly Activity Log

Session 4: What It Means to Be a Man

a. One new thing I learned today was _____

b. This information will help me become a better dad because _____

c. The "Action Steps" I need to take are:

1. _____

2. _____

3. _____

4. _____

FATHERING HANDBOOK • SESSION 5: SPIRITUALITY AND GROWTH

Session 5
Spirituality and Growth

One way men differ from women spiritually is

_____

_____

_____.

One way men and women are alike spiritually is

_____

_____

_____.

How does the American view of masculinity affect men's spirituality?

Spirituality is an important human need for the purpose of feeling membership, attachment, and purpose of life.

Ways to Build Spirituality

1. **Take time for yourself.** It is important to take time during the day and week to do things that lead to your positive health.

2. **Keep a journal.** Write down thoughts and feelings a few times a month about the events in your life. It's neat to look back and see how you've changed.

3. **Exercise.** A healthy body leads to a healthy sense of spirituality.

4. **Read.** Stimulate your imagination, knowledge, and creativity.

5. **Meditate.** Find a place in your mind to go to relax.

6. **Be positive.** Communication has a ripple effect. Be positive and create positive ripples.

7. **Eat and sleep well.** The body needs nourishment. Keep it healthy.

8. **Develop positive relationships.** Choose to be with people who have a positive influence on you.

9. **Support a cause.** Rally around a cause and make the world a better place to live in.

10. **Volunteer.** Giving of your time and energy is a spiritual commitment to life.

11. **Go for walks.** Not only is walking good for your heart, it's good for your soul.

Family Spirituality Checklist

Rate your family's spirituality in the categories below as your family (you, your wife/partner, and your children) are today and where you would like your family to be. Please use the following **rating scale** to respond to the statements:

1   Very Weak
2   Somewhat
3   Average
4   Above Average
5   Very Strong

	We Are Today	We Need to Become
1. Family members communicate with each other.		
2. Compliments are given freely.		
3. We touch each other in affection.		
4. We do things together as a family.		
5. Family members feel free to negotiate and compromise.		
6. Our family has traditions.		
7. Holidays are spent together.		
8. We eat dinner as a family.		
9. Vacations are fun times as a family.		
10. Members are respectful to one another.		

One thing I can begin to do right away to build our family spirituality is: _____

_____

_____

_____.

FATHERING HANDBOOK • SESSION 5: SPIRITUALITY AND GROWTH

The 24/7 Dad examines his thoughts, feelings, and actions on a daily basis to ensure that his actions respect himself, others, and his environment. When the 24/7 Dad discovers his actions might have been disrespectful, the proper course of action to take is to apologize for acting disrespectfully and to be mindful of his future behavior. The posture (the way in which you hold your body) required for this to occur is "openness to change."

Postures of Acceptance to Change

1. "Fight or Flight" Posture

This is the posture of defense and attack. When someone suggests change, the person gets into a "fight or flight" mindset.

Some examples of "Fight or Flight" posture are when someone blames, becomes angry, ignores the need for change, criticizes, starts a fight, or leaves the scene.

Example (Criticize):
"You know Fred, you're never around at night to help put the kids to sleep. I really need your help."

"Well, if you were more organized, you wouldn't need my help. The problem with you is ..."

2. Defensive/Closed Posture

This is the posture of the child. When someone suggests change, the person closes up. Some examples of a "Defensive/Closed" posture are when someone withdraws, becomes stubborn or silent, denies the need for change, or makes excuses.

Example (Excuse):
"You know Fred, you're never around at night to help put the kids to sleep. I really need your help."

"I don't ever remember you asking me for help. Am I a mind reader?"

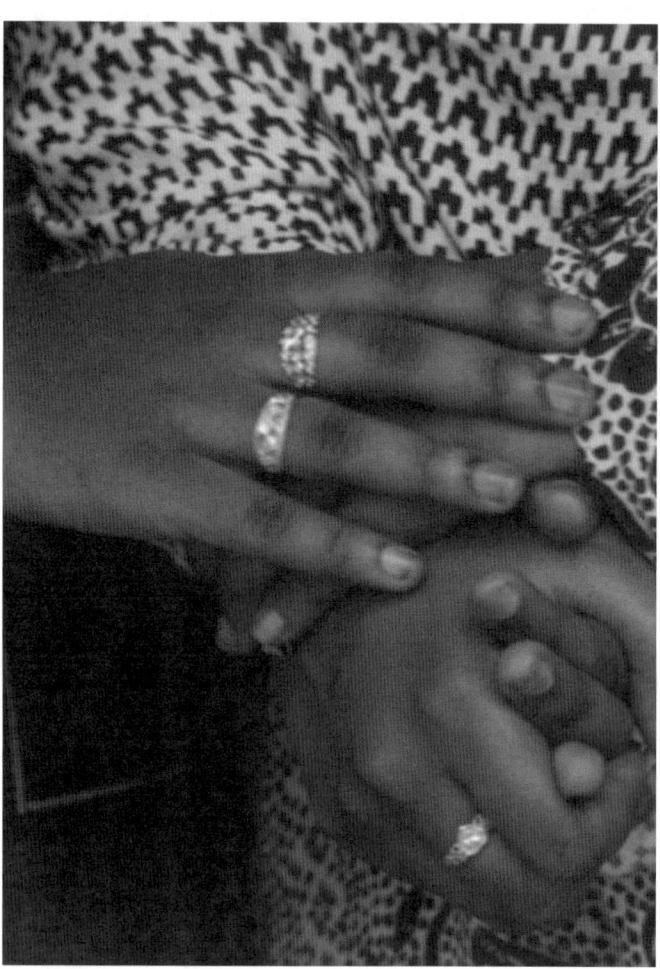

3. Open for Change Posture

This is the posture of the 24/7 Dad. When someone suggests change, the person is willing to listen to the need for change.

Some examples of an "Open for Change" posture are when someone makes eye contact (in some cultures, but not in others), looks

interested, has a pleasant tone, asks questions, wants to help, and seeks to clarify the need for change.

Example (Pleasant Tone and Asks Question): "You know Fred, you're never around at night to help put the kids to sleep. I really need your help."

"I'm sorry. I haven't been available to help you. Let's make a plan. What can we do to work together?"

The most critical factors to being "open to change" are:

1. **Valuing the need to change.** The changes need to have worth before sincere efforts can be made.

2. **Valuing the other person.** If suggestions or observations come from a person who holds little value, the comments will seem more like nagging.

3. **Be mindful.** Be aware of your thoughts and feelings, how you come across to the other person, the mood of the person you are talking with, the situation. These will all help you best judge how to respond.

4. **Know how to change.** Having the right skills or the "know how" to change is an art and a science, and will help the change itself.

Practice the "open for change" posture with your children and wife/partner.

Weekly Activity Log

Session 5: Spirituality and Growth

a. One new thing I learned today was _____
   _____
   _____
   _____

b. This information will help me become a better dad because _____
   _____
   _____
   _____

c. The "Action Steps" I need to take are:

   1. _____
      _____

   2. _____
      _____

   3. _____
      _____

   4. _____
      _____

Session 6

Sex, Love, & Relationships

To me, the difference between sex and love is

_____

_____

_____.

To me, the difference between sex and sexuality is_____

_____

_____.

The quality that sex brings to a relationship is

_____

_____

_____.

The quality that love brings to a relationship is

_____

_____

_____.

Self-Worth

Self-worth is the value men have toward themselves. It includes thoughts (self-concept) and feelings (self-esteem).

Sexual Self-Worth

Sexual self-worth refers to the thoughts and feelings men have about themselves as sexual beings. It includes sexual identity, sexuality, body image, touch, intimacy, physical sexual response, responsibility, health, respect, and trust.

Sexual Identity
Relates to feelings of masculinity.

Sexuality
The things related to being a sexual person, such as appearance, clothes, smell, and image.

Body Image
The positive or negative images people have of their body.

Touch
Related to sexual self-worth - the ability to give and receive sexual and intimate touch.

Intimacy
The feeling of closeness shared in emotional, intellectual, spiritual, and sexual communication.

Physical Sexual Response
The ability to become sensually aroused and achieve orgasm.

Responsibility
Being sexually responsible means preventing the spread of sexually transmitted diseases (STD's), HIV, and unwanted pregnancies.

FATHERING HANDBOOK • SESSION 6: SEX, LOVE & RELATIONSHIPS

Health
Physically being free from sexually transmitted diseases (STDs), practicing sexual abstinence until marriage, and emotionally being a loving partner.

Respect
Respecting your partner's sexual willingness and desires.

Trust
The feeling of risk related to sharing physical, intellectual, emotional, spiritual, and sexual intimacy.

Rating Scale:
1 = very little comfort
2 = average feeling of comfort
3 = feeling very comortable

Sexual Self-Worth Inventory

	1 Low	2 Avg	3 High
1. How comfortable do you feel with your masculinity?			
2. How comfortable do you feel with your sexuality (being a sexual male)?			
3. How comfortable do you feel with the image of your body?			
4. How comfortable do you feel with your ability to give and receive intimacy (a feeling of closeness)?			
5. How comfortable do you feel with your ability to share intimacy?			
6. How comfortable do you feel with your ability to become sexually aroused?			
7. How comfrotable do you feel wih being a responsible sexual being?			
8. How comfortable do you feel with your decisions in keeping yourself sexually and physically healthy?			
9. How comfortable do you feel in your ability to be respectful of your partner's sexual willingness and desires?			
10. How comfortable do you feel in your ability to risk sharing yourself sexually?			

First Edition ©2004 National Fatherhood Initiative

www.fatherhood.org

To Score
1. Add up the numbers you checked.
2. Divide your sum by 10.
3. A score of 1.0 to 1.4 indicates a very low comfort level.
   A score of 1.5 to 1.8 indicates a low/average comfort level.
   A score of 1.9 to 2.2 indicates an average comfort level.
   A score of 2.3 to 2.6 indicates an above average comfort level.
   A score of 2.7 to 3.0 indicates a very high comfort level.

People have always looked for positive relationships that have love and meaning. It is a basic human need to give and receive love from birth to death.

For me, the two most important traits of a loving and positive adult relationship are _____

_____ and _____

_____.

What are the strengths of the relationship you currently have with your wife/partner (or would like to have with a future wife/partner)?
_____
_____
_____
_____
_____

What areas need to be worked on to improve your relationship (or that you need to work on for success in a future relationship)?_____
_____
_____
_____
_____

What is one thing you can do right away to improve your relationship (or prepare for a future relationship)? _____

FATHERING HANDBOOK · SESSION 6: SEX, LOVE & RELATIONSHIPS

Weekly Activity Log

Session 6: Sex, Love, & Relationships

a. One new thing I learned today was _____
   _____
   _____
   _____

b. This information will help me become a better dad because _____
   _____
   _____
   _____

c. The "Action Steps" I need to take are:

   1. _____
      _____

   2. _____
      _____

   3. _____
      _____

   4. _____
      _____

Session 7
Power & Control

To me, having control in my life means _____
_____
_____
_____
_____.

One area of my life I would like to have more control in is _____
_____

because _____
_____
_____.

Power
Power is the ability to exert strength or force on something or someone. Power has to do with a man's physical, mental, and spiritual strength. Power can come with a man's position in life, such as with his job, and can be used in positive and negative ways.

Control
Control is the ability to direct, restrain, or influence your own and others' feelings, emotions, and life. Men sometimes use their power to control others, which includes using their position in life to control others.

Power & Control Inventory

In my role as a Dad, the ways I use my power in positive ways are:

_____
_____
_____
_____

In my role as a Dad, the ways I use my power in negative ways are:

_____
_____
_____
_____

FATHERING HANDBOOK • SESSION 7: POWER AND CONTROL

As a Dad, the positive ways I control my children are:

_____
_____
_____
_____
_____

As a Dad, the negative ways I control my children are:

_____
_____
_____
_____

As a husband/partner, the ways I use my power in positive ways are:

_____
_____
_____
_____
_____

As a husband/partner, the ways I use my power in negative ways are:

_____
_____
_____

How does it feel to want something you can't have?

How does it feel when you prevent someone from having something they really want?

How can you reduce power struggles between yourself and your children?

How can you reduce power struggles between yourself and your wife/partner?

Weekly Activity Log

Session 7: Power & Control

a. One new thing I learned today was _____
_____
_____
_____

b. This information will help me become a better dad because _____
_____
_____
_____

c. The "Action Steps" I need to take are:

    1. _____
_____

    2. _____
_____

    3. _____
_____

    4. _____
_____

FATHERING HANDBOOK • SESSION 8: COMPETITION AND FATHERING

Session 8
Competition & Fathering

What competition means to me is _____
_____
_____ .

What I like about competition is _____
_____

because _____
_____ .

What I don't like about competition is _____
_____

because _____
_____ .

Competitive Vs. Non-Competitive Fathering

Put a check mark by the characteristic that is "more like me" in each of the following categories.

1. Sports
   _____ a. Win at all costs
   _____ b. Have fun; improve skills

2. Grades
   _____ a. Straight As
   _____ b. Study hard; do the best you can

3. Achievement
   _____ a. Never be satisfied
   _____ b. Take pride in accomplishment and pride in yourself for your efforts

4. Possessions
   _____ a. Bigger, better, faster, more expensive
   _____ b. Functional, useful, practical

5. Parenting
   _____ a. Always right; authoritative
   _____ b. Democratic

6. Relationships
   _____ a. Need to be in control
   _____ b. Shares control

7. Efforts
   _____ a. More outcomes oriented
   _____ b. More process oriented

8. Career
   _____ a. Strives to move up at the expense of job satisfaction and family time
   _____ b. Advancement not as important as job satisfaction and time with family

28 First Edition ©2004 National Fatherhood Initiative   www.fatherhood.org

Answers with letter a. indicate a competitive style. Answers with letter b. indicate a non-competitive style.

A more competitive approach to fathering can have its roots in early childhood when Dads failed to achieve something as boys. For example, a Dad who got injured and had to quit playing football in high school encourages his son to play even when his son doesn't want to play.

One regret I have from my childhood about something that I wasn't able to do or accomplish is _____
_____
_____
_____.

One way this regret has influenced my fathering is _____
_____
_____
_____.

Has this experience influenced your values of what girls and boys can do? If so, how?

Has this experience influenced your relationship with your wife/partner? If so, how?

Has this experience influenced your career goals and those of your children? If so, how?

On a scale of 1 to 5 (1 = low; 5 = high) to what degree do you live vicariously through your children? _____

(Living "vicariously" through someone else means that you treat another's experience as if it were your own. For example, you try to push your child to participate in a sport that you loved as a child, but that your child doesn't like. When your child is on the field, it's as if you are on the field living your child's experience.)

In which area or areas of your life is this most evident? _____
_____
_____

How has this influenced the quality of your relationship with your son/daughter/children?
_____
_____
_____

How has this played a role in your relationship with your wife/partner?
_____
_____
_____

Weekly Activity Log

Session 8: Competition and Fathering

a. One new thing I learned today was _____

b. This information will help me become a better dad because _____

c. The "Action Steps" I need to take are:

   1. _____

   2. _____

   3. _____

   4. _____

Session 9
Improving My Communication Skills

My strength in communication is _____
_____
_____
_____
_____ .

My weakness in communication is _____
_____
_____
_____
_____ .

Criticism vs. Confrontation

Criticism leaves a person feeling badly about himself or herself. The person feels worthless, terrible, and inadequate as an entire person. Confrontation leaves a person knowing they have done something you don't like, but they still feel positive about themselves. The difference between criticism and confrontation is the feelings the person is left with. Criticism uses blaming "You Messages."

Examples:

Criticism
"You're such a nag. You're always yelling at me about not helping out."

Confrontation
"I feel upset when you yell at me because it makes me feel foolish and worthless. What I need is for you to ask me in a calm voice when you want my help."

How do you feel when you're criticized?
_____
_____
_____

How do you feel when you're confronted?
_____
_____
_____
_____

Is one easier to take than the other?

Four Steps Involved in Negotiation

Step 1
Determine if there is a difference of opinion.

Dad: "Son, you and I seem to disagree on what time we should create as your curfew."

Step 2
State your views and the views of the other person.

Dad: "I believe curfew should be 8:00 at night on weekdays. In my view, that gives you plenty of time to be with your friends. But you feel that you should be able to stay out until 9:00 because you're the only one coming in so early."

Step 3
Get Clarity.

Dad: "Do I understand what the problem is?"

Step 4
Compromise

Dad: "I can see how you might feel a little funny being the only one coming in at 8:00. Tell you what, how about 8:15?"

Son: "That's still too early. How about 8:45?"

Dad: "Too late. How about if we compromise and say 8:30?"

Son: "Okay, I'll come in at 8:30. Other kids have to be in then, too."

Problem Solving & Negotiation

Problem Solving and Negotiation are two very important skills in communication.
When parents and children have different ideas on what to do, what to wear, when to come home, etc., conversations usually stall. When this happens, both parties feel frustrated and the discussion often leads to arguments. The goal is to reach a settlement while leaving both parties with power. Problem solving and negotiating will leave both parents and children feeling satisfied.

What is an issue that is currently a problem between you and your child/children?

_____

_____

_____

_____

There is a difference between problem solving and decision-making.

Problem Solving
What you do when you have a problem, but don't know what the solution is.

Decision Making
What you do when you know what your options are.

Solving problems can be a person process (something a person does on his/her own) or a family process (where all family members help solve the problem). To take action in solving problems, you need to use the following steps.

Six Steps to Problem Solving

Step 1 Identify the problem.
Write the problem down for you or other family members to see. The first step is an important one. Work on only one problem at a time. Have all family members agree on "the problem."

Step 2 Determine who owns the problem.
Is someone doing something you don't approve of, but does not see the behavior as a problem? Is the problem yours or someone else's? Determine who owns the problem.

Step 3 Discuss what you have tried.
Talk with the person involved with the problem and review past efforts on solving the problem. Remember to use "I Statements" rather than blaming "You Messages."

Step 4 Write down a goal statement.
What behavior do you want to see instead? This is the most crucial step and perhaps the hardest of them all. If it is a family member's problem, tell him or her the behavior you would like to see instead. Discuss the behavior you would like to see instead, and make sure the behavior can be done. Write down what you want to see, not what you don't want to see.

Step 5 Brainstorm ways to achieve what you would like to see instead.
Whether it is your problem or someone else's, brainstorm ways to get the behavior. This is an important step in solving problems.

Step 6 Make a decision. Pick out your favorite three and use them to work on the desired behavior.
From the brainstormed ideas, the decision should be clear. If not, check the problem statement and the goal statement to make certain they still reflect what you mean. If the problem still exists, begin the process with Step 1 again.

When this process does not resolve the issue, family members should use negotiation and compromise. Negotiation and compromise are used in all aspects of society.

Some examples where negotiation and compromise are used are in sports between players and owners over salaries; in buying a car; between governments in arms control; and between union and management.

Weekly Activity Log

Session 9: Improving My Communication Skills

a. One new thing I learned today was _____

b. This information will help me become a better dad because _____

c. The "Action Steps" I need to take are:

   1. _____

   2. _____

   3. _____

   4. _____

Session 10
Having Fun and Getting Involved

(If you grew up with your Dad) One memory I have of my Dad and I having fun is _____

_____

_____.

(If you grew up without your Dad) One way that I hoped to have fun with my Dad was _____

_____

_____.

Ways my Dad (or another "father figure" in my life) and I would play and enjoy being together were _____

_____

_____.

Many Dads find it hard to have fun with their children. Examples:

"You won't catch me acting like a kid."

"Having fun and acting like a kid is acting foolish."

"You won't catch me crawling around on the floor acting silly."

Why do some Dads feel this way?

Negative Aspects of Humor, Laughter, and Fun Include...

Negative Humor
Humor that pokes fun at others; humor at the expense of others.

Negative Laughter
Laughter that pokes fun at others; laughing at the expense of others. (Example: Laughing when someone falls down.)

Negative Fun
Destructive actions or words aimed at physically or emotionally hurting others. (Examples: Tickling a child and not stopping at the child's request; pushing a child in the water.)

Positive Ways to have Fun with Children as a Part of Fathering Include...

Reverse Psychology
In a happy and playful way, request the very behaviors you don't want. (Example: "Okay, I don't want to see anyone getting ready for bed. You have to sit there and not put your pj's on." Or, "I bet none of you guys can beat me up and stairs and get ready for bed!" Make it fun and watch the kids try to beat Dad up the stairs (the kids win).

Fooler Approach
This approach attempts to fool kids into learning the right behavior. (Example: "I bet I can fool you guys. I bet nobody here can brush their teeth all by themselves. No way – you guys can't do it!" Or, "I bet I can fool you guys. I bet nobody here knows our family rule about sharing things. I know it! Everybody is supposed to keep things and not share. Right?" Of course,

FATHERING HANDBOOK • SESSION 10: HAVING FUN & GETTING INVOLVED

the kids yell out "No! Everyone is supposed to share things!" Dad then says, "Well, I sure couldn't fool you kids!") Kids love this game because they get to tell Dad he's wrong.

Talking Objects
Talking objects are a great way to get young kids to cooperate. (Example: Talking bathtub: "Oh Jessica, it's time to jump inside me and get nice and clean." Or, how about a piece of candy or a dessert that says, "No, no don't eat me now. Eat me after supper!")

Ways that I have increased my involvement in my children's lives are _____

_____.

The major benefit of this increased involvement is _____

_____

_____

_____.

"Ways Dads Can Be Involved" Checklist

Make a check mark by the level of involvement you think you show for each example.

1. Being a daily parent.

   _____   _____   _____   _____
   None   A Little   Often   A Lot

2. Attending parent-teacher conferences.

   _____   _____   _____   _____
   None   A Little   Often   A Lot

3. Attending children's events (dance, sports, etc.).

   _____   _____   _____   _____
   None   A Little   Often   A Lot

4. Reading stories to your children.

   _____   _____   _____   _____
   None   A Little   Often   A Lot

5. Helping your children with their homework.

   _____   _____   _____   _____
   None   A Little   Often   A Lot

6. Making meals for your children.

   _____ _____ _____ _____
   None   A Little Often   A Lot

7. Doing outdoor projects with your children.

   _____ _____ _____ _____
   None   A Little Often   A Lot

8. Gardening with your children.

   _____ _____ _____ _____
   None   A Little Often   A Lot

9. Bedtime stories and tucking in your children.

   _____ _____ _____ _____
   None   A Little Often   A Lot

10. Diapering or dressing your children.

    _____ _____ _____ _____
    None   A Little Often   A Lot

11. Playing games with your children.

    _____ _____ _____ _____
    None   A Little Often   A Lot

12. Taking your kids to work for a day.

    _____ _____ _____ _____
    None   A Little Often   A Lot

13. Meeting and knowing your children's friends and their parents.

    _____ _____ _____ _____
    None   A Little Often   A Lot

14. Talking with your children about their interests.

    _____ _____ _____ _____
    None   A Little Often   A Lot

15. Asking your children how their day went.

    _____ _____ _____ _____
    None   A Little Often   A Lot

This list doesn't include every possible way Dads can be involved with their children.. What other ways can you think of?

Weekly Activity Log

Session 10: Having Fun & Getting Involved

a. One new thing I learned today was _____

b. This information will help me become a better dad because _____

c. The "Action Steps" I need to take are:

   1. _____

   2. _____

   3. _____

   4. _____

Session 11

Stress, Alcohol, & Work

When my children become adults, I would be very happy if they handle stress the way I do.

Yes ___   No ___

Why or why not? _____
_____
_____
_____.

When I feel stressed, I usually resort to _____
_____
_____
_____
_____.

One way stress harms my health is _____
_____
_____
_____
_____.

Stress and Alcohol Quiz

Indicate whether you think each statement is a Myth or a Fact.

1. Drinking alcohol reduces your stress.

   _____   _____
   Myth   Fact

2. Stress causes alcoholism.

   _____   _____
   Myth   Fact

3. People don't know when they are addicted to alcohol.

   _____   _____
   Myth   Fact

4. You can inherit alcoholism.

   _____   _____
   Myth   Fact

5. Alcoholism can be cured.

   _____   _____
   Myth   Fact

6. Women should not drink if they are pregnant.

   _____   _____
   Myth   Fact

Answers to Stress and Alcohol Quiz

1. Drinking alcohol reduces your stress.
Myth and Fact. Alcohol in small amounts might lessen the body's response to stress. Studies show, however, that alcohol increases stress by causing the body to produce the same hormones the body produces under stress.

2. Stress causes alcoholism.
Myth. Stress does not cause alcoholism, but problem drinking is linked to stress.

3. People don't know when they are addicted to alcohol.
Myth. There are symptoms that clearly indicate problem drinking. Two common symptoms are lots of drinking after an argument with your wife/partner, when your boss gives you a difficult time, or when you feel under pressure.

4. You can inherit alcoholism.
Fact. Alcoholism runs in families. Genes the person inherits and lifestyle both play a factor. But not all children of alcoholics become alcoholic. And some people can become alcoholics even though no one in their family has a drinking problem.

5. Alcoholism can be cured.
Myth. Alcoholism can't be cured at this time. Even if an alcoholic hasn't been drinking for a long time, he can suffer a relapse. To guard against a relapse, an alcoholic must avoid all drinks with alcohol.

6. Women shouldn't drink if they are pregnant.
Fact. Drinking during pregnancy is dangerous. Fetal Alcohol Syndrome (FES) is mental retardation that is caused from drinking during pregnancy. Alcohol use lowers a man's sperm count, which can lead to problems in trying to have children.

"It's a Man's World"

So often the phrase "It's a Man's World" is used to describe our society. But the facts are, studies on men's health, happiness, and survival simply show this is not true.

- Men live an average of six to seven years less than women.
- Leading fatal diseases target men more often than women.
- Men are the main victims of crime, violence, and murder.
- Most of the people killed or hurt badly on the job are men.
- Men are far more likely to become become addicted to alcohol and other drugs.
- More men than women commit suicide.
- More boys have anxiety, behavior, and mental problems than girls.
- Many men have sexual problems, (i.e. impotence).
- Men are less likely to attend and graduate from college than women.
- The majority of homeless people are single adult men.

Why do men struggle with so many social, economic, and health issues?

One of the major causes of illness in males is stress in the workplace. There is a clear link between stress at work and ill health.

Good Stress vs. Bad Stress (Distress)

There are two types of stress:

Good Stress
Good stress results from pressure that people thrive in to achieve positive actions.

Distress (Bad Stress)
Distress results from too much pressure and too many demands and causes negative actions.

The type of stress I have (had) in my job is _____
_____
_____
_____
_____.

This stress results (resulted) from _____
_____
_____
_____
_____.

The way I handle (handled) this stress is (was)
_____
_____
_____
_____
_____.

How has stress at work had a negative effect on your family life?

How can you learn to manage your stress at work?

Weekly Activity Log

Session 11: Stress, Alcohol, & Work

a. One new thing I learned today was _____
    _____
    _____
    _____
    _____

b. This information will help me become a better dad because _____
    _____
    _____
    _____
    _____

c. The "Action Steps" I need to take are:

    1. _____
        _____

    2. _____
        _____

    3. _____
        _____

    4. _____
        _____

Session 12

Growth & Celebration

One change I've noticed in myself since beginning this program is _____

_____

_____

_____.

Five new fathering skills I have learned as a result of participating in this group are:

1. _____

2. _____

3. _____

4. _____

5. _____

Weekly Activity Log

Session 12: Growth & Celebration

a. One new thing I learned today was _____
   _____
   _____
   _____

b. This information will help me become a better dad because _____
   _____
   _____
   _____

c. The "Action Steps" I need to take are:

   1. _____
      _____

   2. _____
      _____

   3. _____
      _____

   4. _____
      _____